100 Parables Of Zen

ASIAPAC COMIC SERIES

100 Parables Of Zen
百喻經

Illustrated by N S Chen
Translated by Joyce Lim

ASIAPAC • SINGAPORE

Publisher
ASIAPAC BOOKS PTE LTD
629 Aljunied Road #04-06
Cititech Industrial Building
Singapore 1438
Tel: 7453868
Fax: 7453822

First published February 1995

©ASIAPAC BOOKS, 1995
ISBN 981-3029-49-8

Cover design by NS Chen
Typeset by Quaser Technology Pte Ltd
Body text in 8/9 Futura Book
Printed in Singapore by Chung Printing

Publisher's Note

100 Parables of Zen contains 98 humorous yet philosophical stories compiled from the sutras. Through the silly behaviour and antics of so-called fools, one can learn some valuable lessons of life. For instance, in *Killing the Guide*, we learn that "a short-term solution only conceals a crisis and causes an even bigger difficulty". In another story, *Dividing the Spoils*, we see that "something that is unfortunate may prove to be a blessing in disguise". In *The Mercenary Man*, we see how the materialistic world is full of scheming people who flatter and fawn on the rich, hoping to gain something in return.

We may laugh along with the absurd stories but at a deeper level, these parables are food for thought to reflect on our own lives and act as a means to keep our morals in check. We hope you'll find this book enlightening yet entertaining.

About the Illustrator

N S Chen is the creative director of an advertising firm in Singapore. With about thirty years of experience in advertising, Chen has worked with internationally renowned firms such as Ogilvy & Mather and Mccann-Erickson.

Chen won the championship in the National Logo Design Contest in 1982. He is not only adept in commercial design, but also in illustrations. His simple yet interesting line drawings have been published and well received in various media.

Eating Salt
愚人吃盐

A fool was invited to his friend's house for dinner.

The host quickly added some salt to the food.

Storing Milk for Later Use
傻瓜藏奶

A man decided to save some milk for use at a feast one month later.

If I were to milk the cow every day, I would run out of storage space in no time. Besides, the milk would turn sour.

Hitting A Bald-headed Man with Pears

梨打秃头

A man was always battered on the head with pears by people.

Even when his head bled, he did not move an inch.

Man is quick to detect the folly of others but cannot see his own shortcomings.

Believing in a Lie

妇人诈死

There was a man who loved his pretty wife very much.

But the woman had an affair with another man and planned to elope with him.

Auntie, after I've left, please find a corpse and place it on my bed. Tell my husband I've died.

Looking for Water
呆子找水

A fool who was very thirsty looked desperately for water.

He saw some steam coming out of the ground and thought it was water. When he went closer and realised his mistake, he was very angry.

After much difficulty, he finally found a river. Instead of drinking the water, he simply stared at it.

11

Killing His Sons to Balance the Pole

杀子成双

There was a fool who had seven sons.
When one of them died suddenly,
his corpse was left at home.

12

The Mercenary Man
认财作兄

There was once a good-looking man
who was both clever and rich.

A fool claimed that he was related to the rich man, hoping to benefit from the rich man's influence.

He's my brother.

The world is full of people who fawn on the rich in the hope of gaining benefits.

Stealing the King's Clothes

野人偷衣

After robbing the king's treasure house, a wild man fled as far away as he could.

Not long after, he was caught and brought before the king.

Why did you steal my clothes?

My Father is the Greatest

爸爸万岁

The Mirage

海市蜃楼

A silly rich man paid his friend a visit
and became very envious of his friend's
three-storey house. He decided to build
a similar house for himself.

Killing His Son to Save His Reputation

杀子盗名

There was a Brahmin who was learned and good at fortune-telling. He took his son with him to another country to show off his talent.

According to my prediction, my son will die in a week's time.

Why are you crying so sadly?

When the seventh day came and the boy still did not die, the Brahmin killed him to prove that his prediction was accurate.

He can really foretell the future!

You're fantastic!

*A Brahmin is a Hindu of the highest caste.

Many rulers are no better than false prophets.

Fanning the Soup to Cool It

扬汤止沸

A man was cooking some black rock honey....

A rich man came to visit him...

I should serve him some dessert.

24

Quick to Anger

闻过则怒

Killing the Guide

杀死响导

A group of traders decided to travel to another land for business.

They hired a guide to show them the way.

One day, they passed by a temple.

Growing up in the Blink of an Eye
瞬间长大

Watering a Plant with its Juice

蔗汁浇蔗

33

Penny Wise, Pound Foolish

因小失大

A trader once lent half
a unit of cash to a friend.

After some time, when the
friend still did not repay
him, the trader decided to
look for him for payment.

How much does
it cost to cross
the river?

Two units
of cash.

What rotten luck! Nobody's at home.

Boatman, I want to cross the river.

That'll be two units of cash.

After a long journey by boat, the trader finally reached home exhausted, without collecting his debt...

Thrift is often just an excuse for one to be selfish and mean.

Moving a Camel to the Grindstone

就石磨刀

To sharpen the knife, the man kept going up and down the stairs. He soon got exhausted.

What a fool I've been! I should have moved the camel upstairs.

It's more convenient now.

It is unwise to just consider immediate gains without any regard for others' feelings.

Retrieving a Lost Bowl from the Sea

画纹求盂

Once, a man travelling in a boat accidentally dropped a silver bowl into the river.

I'll make a mark here and retrieve the bowl later.

Two months later, he came to a country called Shizhi.

When he spotted a river, he immediately dived into the water.

Losing 100 and Being Compensated 1,000

索百补千

*1 *liang* = 50 grams

41

Sacrificing a Son to Gain Another
杀子求子

A woman who has just given birth to a son wanted to have another.

Please tell me how I can have another son soon.

Simple. Just worship Heaven.

43

Burning Aloes Wood

火烧沉香

A man went out to sea to gather aloes wood.

This is all the wood I've managed to gather after more than a year of hard work. They are very precious.

If I sell them in the market, I'll surely make a lot of money.

45

Wrapping Old Clothes with Silk

绸裹破衣

Once, a thief sneaked into a rich man's home.

47

Cooking the Linseeds
炒熟种子

49

The Changeable Elements
水火无常

There was once a man who needed both cold water and fire to do his job.

Let me put this basin of cold water over the fire. Not only will it save space but it will also be more convenient.

Imitating Others Blindly

东施效颦

Healing One's Wounds with Horse Dung
马粪敷伤

Changing the Wife's Nose

为妻换鼻

There was a man whose wife was very beautiful except for her nose.

What a lovely nose that woman's got. Let me cut it off and fix it onto my wife's face!

57

Burning Clothes to Have New Ones
穷人烧衣

A poor man found a woollen garment near a well one day.

He wore it over his clothes.

Okay!

You look like a rich man. Why are you wearing such old clothes? Let me teach you a way to get some new clothes.

Fooled by a Swindler
牧人受骗

There was a very miserly goatherd who would not give away any goats.

One day he met a swindler.

I know of a girl from a good family. Let me propose marriage to her on your behalf.

61

The Donkey that Breaks Pottery

笑驴破陶

63

Using Cotton to Keep Gold

棉花裹金

There were two traders.
One sold gold and
the other sold cotton.

65

Felling a Tree for its Fruit

砍树摘果

The mercenary man only thinks of immediate gains with little thought for the consequences.

Transporting Water
傻瓜送水

200 *li* from the capital was a village well-known for its sweet mineral water. The king ordered the villagers to send water to the capital every day.

To avoid being conscripted to carry water, the villagers decided to move to another town.

He who is too trusting
often gets shortchanged.

The Man in the Mirror

镜中藏人

A poor man who was heavily
in debt was constantly
on the run.

Oh?!
There's
a chest!

One day, he fled to the wilderness.

A man who has done something wrong fears his own image.

Gouging Out the Eyes

挖取天眼

There was a man who was blessed with the Five Gifts*. He had a pair of special eyes that could see treasures buried in the ground.

If we can make him stay in our country, we'll be rich.

What's so difficult about that?

Aahh!

*The Five Gifts refer to the gifts of special sight, hearing and other unusual abilities.

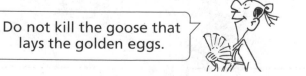

Do not kill the goose that lays the golden eggs.

73

Killing a Herd of Cattle
奢杀牛群

A man had 250 head of cattle.

One day a tiger ate a head of his cattle.

Stopping the Water from Flowing
阻止水流

A man was tired and thirsty after a long walk.

Ah! Water!

I've already quenched my thirst. Why is the water still flowing?

Plastering the Wall with Rice

拿米涂墙

A man went to his friend's house.

How did you make your walls so smooth?

Oh, I plastered my walls with rice bran mixed with mud.

79

Seeking a Cure for Baldness

禿者求医

There was a bald man whose head felt very cold in winter...

and hot in summer.

He always got bitten by mosquitoes and insects on the head and found it hard to get a good night's rest.

Two Quarrelling Ghosts

两鬼相争

Two ghosts bickered constantly over a bamboo chest, a walking stick and a pair of wooden clogs.

A man tried to stop them from quarrelling.

Stop squabbling! What do you see in this stuff anyway?

Using Cotton Cloth to Cover the Camel Skin

氈盖驼皮

A trader brought some fine cotton cloth and valuables with him on a business trip.

Unfortunately, the camel died along the way.

The trader skinned the camel.

I have to go. Look after the goods for me and keep the camel skin dry.

Yes, master.

85

Grinding a Stone to Make a Toy Cow

愚人磨石

A man brought home a huge stone to grind.

He worked at it day and night.

After much grinding, the stone finally became very small.

So much hard work – just to produce a toy cow!

Nothing can be more foolish than wasting one's effort on something trivial.

Filling One's Stomach with Sesame Cakes

饿吃煎饼

He who is wise will not hunger after quick success.

Keeping an Eye on the Door

看好家门

An opera was being staged in a nearby village. The servant wanted to join in the fun.

One must have an overall view of a problem before solving it.

Stealing an Ox

村人偷牛

A group of villagers stole an ox and had a feast after that.

The owner of the ox caught up with them.

Is my ox in your village?

There isn't any village here.

You were feasting on it under a tree by the pond, weren't you?

There isn't any tree or pond here.

92

93

Silence is Not Golden
该叫不叫

A country which was holding an upcoming celebration required all the women to wear clothes and accessories made of lotus flowers.

In the house of a poor family....

Go and get me some lotus flowers or I'll divorce you.

The poor man sneaked into the king's garden to steal the lotus flowers.

I'm good at imitating the call of mandarin ducks. If I'm found out, I'll start calling like one.

The Fox and the Tree
野干看树

A fox was standing under a tree.

A sudden gust of wind snapped off some of the branches of the tree which fell on the fox's back.

The fox immediately ran away.

The Children and Hair from the River
孩童抓毛

Two little boys playing in a river found a bunch of hair.

This is the moustache of an immortal.

This hair belongs to either a man or a bear.

Let's not argue but check with the Immortal.

The Quack Doctor
庸医治病

Five Men and a Maid

婢女洗衣

Five men shared to buy a maid.

Yes, Master Zhou.

Could you please wait a while? I have to wash Master Zhou's robe first.

Wash this for me immediately!

The Singer
歌妓献唱

Breaking the Teacher's Legs

师父断腿

A man had two disciples who were always squabbling.

My legs are giving me trouble. From now on, I want both of you to be in charge of massaging a leg each.

One day, one of the disciples went out.

Hee! Hee! I'll break the leg you're in charge of while you're away!

Ouch!

Ouch!

Do not make others sacrifice for your own selfish gain.

The Tail that Wants to Lead

蛇尾争前

Shaving the King's Moustache

为王剃须

The progressive man aspires to success and is not complacent.

111

Pushing a Cart
愚人推车

113

The Bootlicking Fool

傻瓜拍马

There was a very rich man whom everybody fawned on.

Whenever he spit on the ground, everybody rushed to wipe off his saliva with their feet.

A fool never got a chance to do so.

Got it! I must act faster than everyone else.

115

Fighting Over the Family Property
兄弟争产

A nobleman lay in bed seriously ill.

When I'm gone, you must divide the family property equally between the two of you!

Father!

Father!

Brother, I don't think you've divided the property fairly.

Why?

Stop arguing! Just break everything into two and you will get your fair share!

There is no absolute fairness in this world.

Watching a Potter at Work

观看制陶

Fishing for Gold in the River
水底捞金

121

The Fool's Creations

愚人造物

The Heavenly King was reputed to be the creator of the universe.

What's so great about him? I can create all things too.

Eating Pheasants

愚人吃雉

A man was seriously ill.

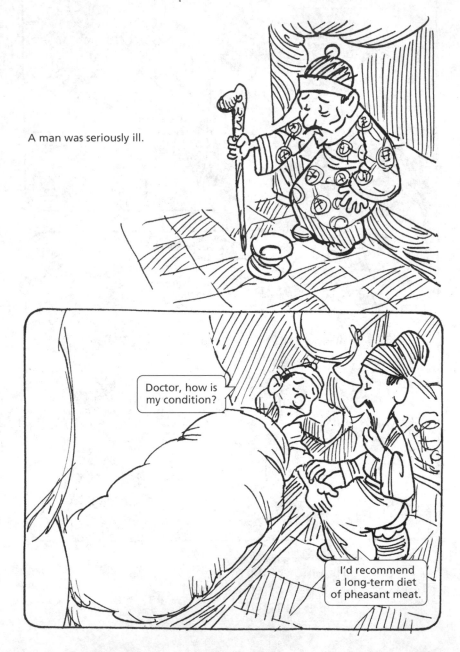

The man only had one meal of pheasant meat and decided that it was enough.

How can you hope to get well just by eating one pheasant?

Doctor, I've already eaten a pheasant. Why hasn't my condition improved?

Good health is not built up overnight.

The Singing Girls and the Ghost

歌妓遇鬼

A group of singing girls left their hometown because of the famine there.

Grr... it's so cold.

One day, they decided to spend the night at a supposedly haunted hill.

It's a good thing we brought this costume along. It keeps me warm!

A ghost?! Help!

Man is often haunted by the "ghosts" in his own heart.

Staying in a Haunted House

寄宿鬼屋

Nobody dared to live in an old house because it was said to be haunted.

129

Blessed are the Foolish

愚人傻福

A loose woman thought of ways and means to kill her husband.

Husband, you can have these tablets on the way.

One day, before her husband set off on a trip, she gave him 500 tablets filled with poison.

I'm setting off now. Take care.

I'll spend the night up in the tree.

Steering a Boat

愚人开船

Among a group of men going out to sea was the son of a nobleman.

Before he set off, he memorised all the methods of steering a boat.

Don't worry. I've learnt how to steer the boat.

Fighting over a Biscuit
夫妻争饼

A man and his wife had three biscuits. After both of them had each taken a biscuit, there was only one left.

The person who talks first forfeits the chance of eating the biscuit.

Fine.

I must keep quiet or I'll lose.

A thief sneaked into the house.

139

The Price of Hatred

仇恨之害

There was a man who was very unhappy because of his feud with another man.

You can always put a curse on your enemy. But before the spell can work, you have to hurt youself.

I don't mind hurting myself as long as I can have my revenge.

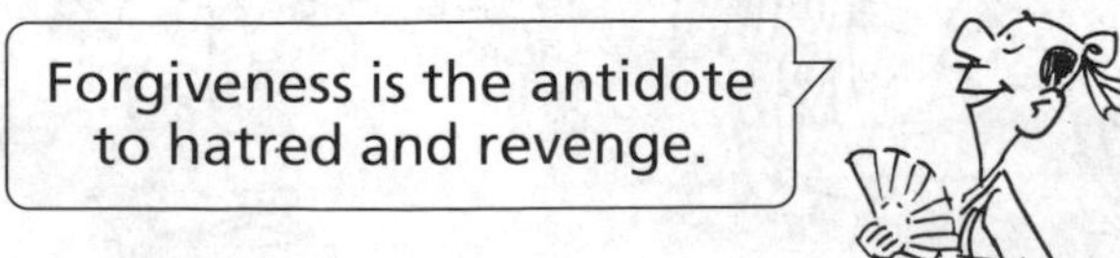
Forgiveness is the antidote to hatred and revenge.

Following the Ancestors' Example
效法祖先

A man travelled from Northern India to Southern India.

Later, he married a local girl.

Tasting Fruits

仆人尝果

145

The Wife and the Concubine

一妻一妾

A man married two wives.

The first wife is angry again.

He agreed to sleep between the two of them.

Even when the rain and soil fell into his eyes, he didn't dare to move.

In the end... he became blind.

You cannot have your cake and eat it.

Stealing Rice and Keeping Quiet

丈夫偷米

A man visited his wife at her parents' home. She was pounding rice.

Strange!

Father, look! His mouth is swollen.

This is strange!

148

149

The Black Horse with a White Tail

黑马白尾

A soldier charged into the enemy's camp on a black horse.

A coward, he quickly lay on the ground and pretended to be dead.

After the enemy had left, he decided to go home. He cut off a white horse's tail to show off to the folks back home.

151

Pretending to Have Bathed

诈言洗净

except for one believer....

Whenever other people poured water into his barrel,

he would pour the water away immediately and act as if he had just taken a bath.

What's there to be afraid of? The law exists in name only.

He who keeps up a false appearance ultimately deceives himself and others.

The Camel's Head Stuck in a Jar

驼头入瓮

Besotted with the Princess

迷恋公主

A farmer went to town on a trip.

157

Milking the Donkey

愚人挤乳

People living along the border did not know what a donkey was but had heard that it produced very fresh milk.

One day, they were given a male donkey.

159

An Unnecessary Trip

白跑一趟

The "smart" boy was soon overcome by exhuastion.

When he finally got home, he had almost died of hunger and thirst.

Because...because... I didn't know what it was that you wanted.

You left without me, why have you come home empty-handed?

Get your target right before you proceed to do anything.

Carrying Stools on the Back

臣子搬凳

The king decided to pay a visit to the Garden of No Worries.

Carry a stool so that I can take a rest whenever I'm tired.

What... carry a stool?!

Too Much Medicine Too Soon

乱喝药物

Every organ has its functions – the natural order cannot be reversed.

Avenging His Son

父报子仇

A father and his son were walking through the woods with some men.

167

Sowing Seeds

愚人撒种

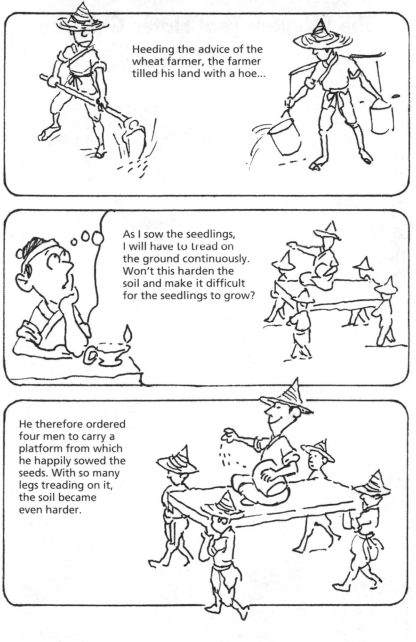

Heeding the advice of the wheat farmer, the farmer tilled his land with a hoe...

As I sow the seedlings, I will have to tread on the ground continuously. Won't this harden the soil and make it difficult for the seedlings to grow?

He therefore ordered four men to carry a platform from which he happily sowed the seeds. With so many legs treading on it, the soil became even harder.

The world is full of fools who like to show off their "intelligence".

The Monkey That Hates Children

猴怨小孩

Help!

A monkey was often
attacked by grown men.

171

The Dog and the Moon

狗吃月亮

An evil deity, jealous of the bright shining moon, deliberately blocked it with his hand. This resulted in an eclipse and the earth was enveloped in darkness.

When the people saw the eclipse, they thought the heavenly dog had eaten up the moon, so they began hitting all the dogs they saw.

The ignorant adhere to ridiculous practices.

Gouging out One's Eyes
挖掉眼睛

The Father who Chops Off His Son's Head

父斩儿头

A father and his son saw bandits riding towards them...

Oh no, the worst has happened...

The father was worried that the bandits would demand his son's gold earring. He tried very hard to yank it off, but it just wouldn't come off.

He managed to save the earring.

The bandits left shortly. The father tried to fix his son's head back but...

Without a sound plan, one is doomed to failure.

177

Dividing the Spoils
强盗分赃

179

The Monkey that Searches for Beans

猕猴觅豆

A monkey was clutching a handful of beans when he dropped one of them.
He threw away all the other beans to look for the lost bean...

He who pursues wealth or power
at all costs will eventually
lose everything.

Crossing the River with a Snake

揣蛇渡河

Ha! Fancy stumbling upon a golden weasel – one made of pure gold. Ha! Ha!

The man held the weasel to his bosom and got ready to cross the river.

The weasel suddenly turned into a poisonous snake, but the man still believed it was a weasel. He continued holding the snake close to his bosom.

The Poor Man who Finds Gold

穷人拾金

Ah! A bag of money!

Overcome with joy, the man proceeded to count the number of ingots.

Throwing Away His Money

穷人弃财

Giving a Child Sweets
小孩吃糖

The Old Woman who is Chased by a Bear

熊追老妇

An old woman was resting under a tree.

The old woman ran round and round the tree.

190

191

A Misundertanding

误解摩尼

A man was having an affair with another man's wife.

Ah!

Quick, excape by the *mani**.

*Mani is a Sanskrit word that means a bead or a drain.

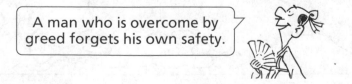

A man who is overcome by greed forgets his own safety.

Killing the Female Pigeon

误杀雌鸽

A pair of pigeons gathered fruits day and night.

Why have the fruits shrunk? Oh Heavens!

You must have eaten some.

I didn't! I didn't!

Destroying His Sight to Avoid Hard Work

工匠毁目

197

Using Gold to Redeem Clothes

以金赎衣

Two men were travelling together in the woods.

Take off your cotton robe!

Return me my robe and I'll give you money!

199

Killing a Tortoise

小孩杀龟

A kid stumbled upon
a big tortoise.

201

《亞太漫畫系列》

百喻經

繪畫：陳彥之
翻譯：林珍珠

亞太圖書有限公司出版